GET THE HELL OVER IT

How to Let Go of Fear and Realize Your Creative Dream

SARAH BETH MOORE

ISBN-13: 978-1548170530

ISBN-10: 1548170534

Publishing services provided by  **Archangel Ink**

Contents

Preface, Or: Let's Get This Thing Going

If you're holding this book in your hand – or, more likely, if your Kindle is holding it in its little electronic brain – then you're probably afraid. Not of plane crashes or zombies or aliens or a Kindle uprising (although I am most assuredly afraid of all of those things) but of creativity. Making. Doing. Sharing. Selling.

The whole awesome, icky shebang that constitutes living and working as a creative in today's ever-shrinking digital world.

If you're like me, you find this simultaneously freeing and terrifying. *Everyone will see everything I do!* you crow. On the other hand ... *EVERYONE WILL SEE EVERYTHING I DO.*

WELL, CRAP.

Because it cuts both ways, right? The internet, social media, telecommuting – these newfangled developments make it easier than ever to get your dreams out there. But at the same time, it is also easier than ever to make a misstep or commit a faux pas or fail spectacularly ... in front of everyone.

Believe me, I know. I've done it again and again and again. And again. And also that one other time. Oh, and yesterday.

... I've done it a lot. Let's just leave it at that.

But no one died, not any of those times. I mean, maybe a little bit of my soul. I'll admit that's happened once or twice. But real death? The kind with funerals? Nada.

The fear lives on, though, doesn't it?

Maria Popova put it best in Brain Pickings: "'Creativity is like chasing chickens,' Christoph Niemann once said. But sometimes it can feel like being chased by chickens – giant, angry, menacing chickens. Whether you're a writer, designer, artist or maker of anything in any medium, you know the creative process can be plagued by fear, often so paralyzing it makes it hard to actually create."

Admit it, *this has happened to you.* Instead of making that sweet, sweet music (or art or literature or sculpture or whatever), you're hunkered in your room, eating your kids' fruit snacks and trying to pretend the chickens aren't there.

But they are. Oh, the chickens are.

The good news is this: You get to choose what to do about it. Obviously, given the title of this here book, I think you should do something badass, like tell fear to kiss off. Fo-evah.

But just how are we going to do that? you're wondering.

Good question. I like questions. Keep 'em coming.

The answer? Well, the title says it all, really:

Get the Hell Over It: How to Let Go of Fear and Realize Your Creative Dream.

Fear of what others will think, combined with the pressure to do something "normal" or "safe" with our lives, has taken many a creative down. We worry. We fret. We tiptoe toward our latest brainchild, then shy away, leaving it sad and alone in the dark.

Without any fruit snacks, even.

We're gonna get you over that, with a combination support system and toolbox for moving past the creative fears that are blocking your ability to realize your passions.

See, the main problem with beginning *any* creative project is that it has so many moving parts the whole thing becomes paralyzing. Instead of taking a methodical step-by-step approach that proceeds from idea to tools to mastery, we begin to flail, trying one halfhearted tactic after another. When those tactics fail over and over, like the world's saddest line of dominoes ... we give up. Because, we figure, that's it.

We just can't do it.

Someone fetch the cheese dip ... let's get this pity party started!

But, come on. That's really no fun at all. So here's your alternative: a handy, down-to-earth, practical guide on how to deal with the natural emotions that accompany creativity and entrepreneurship.

You're welcome.

Now, before we go any further ...

A note on using this guide:

Because I think our dreams are so important, I've included lots and lots of resources in this guide. They come in two forms:

Links.

These are some of my favorite go-tos for inspiration, knowledge, self-work and more. I don't include that many, because I want the ones I *do* put in to be meaningful. I highly recommend you check them out. Good stuff, people.

Exercises.

These require (or if you prefer, *invite*) your participation. You can write your answers down on paper, print out the pertinent pages or, if you have a physical book, photocopy them. (Gasp! Yes, people still do it). It's up to you. Or you can also just think through them; the thought exercises included are all relatively simple and more meant to get your creative juices flowing than to hash out anything specific. So make it your own.

You'll notice throughout this book, in fact, that it's more a primer on how to *think* about creativity than it is a step-by-step guide. I mean, yes, it's that too. But mostly, this book is a recognition of how GD HARD it is to make it as a creative, and that the biggest enemy we face is our own thoughts.

This book is all about telling those thoughts to take a hike.

Immediately.

Before we kill them and turn them into stew.

STEW, I SAY.

And now all that's left is the disclaimer:

This book is not intended to replace therapy, friendship, hard work, research, palm-reading, astrology, personality tests or actual job counseling. I am not responsible for your career choices (though if you become a shooting star, I will be first in line to take credit).

However. You can and should use this ebook to replace emotional eating, crying in the bathtub and wine binges. I want you to stop mourning your dream and start earning it.

I WANT YOU TO GET THE HELL OVER IT ALL.

It is my considered opinion that your vision is worthy and viable, but since we've never met, you'll have to find that out on your own.

Ready?

I know you are. But just in case, I'll leave you with the words of young amazeballs poet Erin Hanson:

"What if I fall? Oh, but my darling, what if you fly?"

See, you totes feel better now, right? Okay then ...

ONWARD!

I.
It's Time to Go for It, Or: I'm Tired of Seeing Our Dreams Fail

If I hear another person bemoan the devaluation of the degree, I might just scream. A high, girly scream that will totally ruin the cup of tea you're trying to enjoy right now.

Okay, yes. It is a fact: College no longer guarantees a career. The American dream of good job, great house, two kids, one puppy, beaucoup martinis and Don Draper hair for all ... is no longer true.

But then, we've known this for a while. The question is, What are we going to do about it?

I'm happy to see that the old-school desire to find a steady job right out of college is giving way to the new-school, ever-more-popular prospect of launching that dream business, working from home, building something out of nothing.

I find myself in this latter camp, as does the ever-expanding class of people who identify with the job description of "creative," a word that, until five or ten years ago, was only ever used as an adjective in the mainstream. I mean, sure, the truly artsy-artsy were using it as a noun before that ... but no one was listening. Probably because of the berets. One assumes.

Anyway, it's no longer true.

Now "creative" *is* a noun, and a kick-ass one at that. Creatives come in all shapes and sizes, from artists and writers to gardeners and carpenters and people who just really like gluing weird shit together.

And no matter what form it takes, creativity is power, wealth, currency.

Partially this is due to the internet, which has afforded liberty and opportunity like never before, allowing anyone with a few hundred bucks and a dream to launch their creative endeavor and succeed. Sites like Etsy, Kickstarter and even PayPal have freed many from the need to make their living feeding someone else's dream and instead live their own.

Partially, too, the explosion of creatives is a result of a world saturated by automation and chintzy, dime-a-dozen goods and services. We are tired of same old, same old, and yearn for simpler, more handmade times.

Uniqueness satisfies this urge.

Retro artwork, hand lettering, vintage finds, personalized experiences of all types are beginning to characterize commerce. Writers now help companies tell "stories" about themselves; wedding invitations are adorned with hand-painted flowers and real calligraphy.

Daniel Pink elaborates on this in his book *A Whole New Mind: Why Right-Brainers Will Rule the Future,* a powerful look at what makes creatives tick and how they can leverage this natural advantage in the coming decades.

In essence, people who can design well, tell great stories, see connections, empathize deeply, create new types of play and impart meaning will become society's new MVPs. They will bring solace to a world scarred and exhausted by the soullessness of the assembly line and the corporation.

But only – and this is a biggie – if you can get the hell over it. Because with all this creativity and boot-strapping and self-made-ness comes the age-old fear of creating, facing judgment and being found wanting.

To which I say: Who cares? We'll discuss this more in Chapter V, when we take a hard look at what failure and fear really mean for your creative career (hint: almost nothing), but for now, just know this:

Your time has come.

Many of us read such proclamations and think "Awesome! I'm a creative! My time has come! She just said so and she would NOT lie to me!"

Here's the thing, though: I might lie to you. You don't really know, do you? You. Just. Don't. Know.

And more to the point, turning a dream into a living is, like, *really hard.*

This is due to many things, but mostly to an over-emphasized and underexamined belief:

Do what you love; the money will come.

Yes. Sort of. You're on your way. If we could just tweak this a *teeny-weeny* little bit. Maybe something along the lines of:

Do what you love (and perform research and make plans and work your butt off and market yourself to the right people and kick fear in the teeth and keep at it for months and years); the money will come.

Okay. That's more like it. See, too many of us (myself, until recently, included) believe the pervasive myth that passion is enough, *but it isn't*. If your passion can't fuel a tremendous amount of work, leap hurdles of self-doubt and withstand the test of time, then your dream may not have what it takes. If your passion can't prompt you to just get the hell over fear and insecurity and create *no matter what*, then it's pretty weak stuff.

But I believe you can do it. The world *is* ready for the uniqueness you have to offer, for your right-brained badassery, and I don't think there's *anything* wrong with your dream.

It's those other parts that are hanging you up: research, planning, practice, marketing, self-belief. A willingness to kill yourself to make it happen. And a decision to just let go of the negative thoughts standing in your way and go for it the way a toy poodle goes for one of those giant, pointy-eared Great Danes. They don't stop to consider what comes next; *they just do it*.

Now obviously, I don't have all the answers, or even most of them. But I've got a journalist's mind and an educator's heart, and between the two I've figured out quite a bit. I'd like to share what I know with you, help you find a way to unkink the questions, unmake the doubts and unlearn all the reasons you can't do this. Because you can.

I'll help you:

- » Recognize the difference between dreams, fantasies and byproducts
- » Get in touch with what really drives you
- » Learn to shoot for the right goal
- » Prioritize your creative urges
- » Get people on board with your dream and dismiss the people who don't support it (nicely, with a smile)
- » Target your market, find your tools and learn your trade
- » Learn to showcase yourself with the right words and design aesthetic
- » Figure out how to figure it all out

I can't make anything happen for you. But I can give you some of my blood, sweat and tears in the form of lessons I've amassed over years of trying to make my own dreams as a writer and artist happen.

I'm finally on the right track, and my hope is that I can help you get there much, much sooner than I did. The truth is, it's really not that hard to turn a dream into a business. By the time you finish reading this ebook, you'll probably feel like you didn't learn that much you didn't already know (double negative, sorry).

So why the hell did I buy it from you, then? you're wondering.

Because this ebook is going to give you permission to believe in a dream that you've always thought was small, silly, unrealistic or unworkable. I'll show you how to turn that little hope into a real, viable business idea, and then build slowly from there in a way that is lasting and measurable. You know how the Empress in *The Neverending Story* shows Bastian the grain of sand that becomes all of Fantasia?

Yeah. It's kinda like that. (If you don't get that reference, stop reading and go watch the movie immediately. I can't *even* talk to you until you do.) And yes, that makes me the Empress ...

Also, it's okay to do all of this slowly and quietly. It's okay to start small. It's okay to do it even if you don't know what you're doing, like I did. Like I'm still doing.

Your dreams are real, and that means they're important. Realizing your creative dream is not only possible, it's likely ... as long as you stick with it. As long as you get the hell over everything that doesn't serve you. Stat.

So come on. Let's do this.

Exercise:

Start by writing down a few of your long-held creative dreams. If you don't have any pre-existing dreams or passions, write down a few creative endeavors you think you might be good at.

II.
What's In a Dream? Or: Fun With Definitions

I'm not great at keyword research. It seems hard and technical and, I don't know, esoteric.

(For anyone who is similarly hopeless, keyword research essentially involves finding words that relate to your subject that people are already searching for online. When you therefore use them in your blog posts, you're more likely to draw traffic. The more specific the keyword, the better. Like, instead of "cats," you might use the keyword "schizophrenia in hairless cats," which I totally bet is a thing. Those f***ers are *weird*.)

In a fit of determination one day a few years ago, I decided to end this helplessness. I was writing a blog post about "goals" and decided a definition would be a good place to start.

It seemed simple enough, but when I put "goal" into the keyword finder, I was totally mystified by the results: "football," "Santiago," "net," "score." As it turns out, I'd performed my search at the height of the World Cup and so predictably was fed a whole bunch of soccer terminology.

But see, that's what I like about definitions:

Sometimes you think you know exactly where you stand with a word, but then you realize you never really saw to the heart of it.

This is particularly true when it comes to dreams.

I think we often daydream about what *could* be, without actually taking the time to make it happen. Or we dream negatively, fantasizing briefly before immediately shutting ourselves down. Or we dream of the wrong things, limiting ourselves without even knowing it.

To dream in the right ways, on the other hand, means to visualize what we want out of life while assuming the best. Assuming we can do it.

And here's where we get to definitions.

"Dream."

"Fantasy."

"Byproduct."

These words are all quite different, but are often conflated under the umbrella heading of "dream." So let's break it down. Stick with me.

Dictionary.com defines "dream" the following ways:

1) "a succession of images, thoughts or emotions passing through the mind during sleep.

2) "the sleeping state in which this occurs.

3) "an object seen in a dream.

4) "an involuntary vision occurring to a person when awake.

5) "a vision voluntarily indulged in while awake; daydream; reverie.

6) "an aspiration; goal; aim: A trip to Europe is his dream.

7) "a wild or vain fancy."

And that's just the nouns. Perhaps most fascinating is the fact that while sleep-related definitions top the list – and "dream" as a synonym for "goal" doesn't appear until No. 6 – they do not account for most uses of the word in popular culture.

The American Dream, for instance. Or Oprah's Dream Board. Or pretty much every blog out there about creativity, passion, right living, career and more.

"Dream" means "goal," but goal in its purest, most highly realized form.

Then there's No. 7, "a wild or vain fancy." In other words, a fantasy. People often mistake fantasies for dreams, but the two are not the same. However lovely your vision may be of hooking up with Ryan Gosling on the rings of Saturn while friendly Martians serve you piña coladas, it is *not* a dream. (But, um, it's still really nice. Also, can I join you?)

The point? In almost all cases, fantasies cannot come true.

Lastly, I would like to distinguish between dreams and byproducts. Folks, myself included, often mistake these as well. "Write a book," "Start a handmade soap business" and "Hike K2" are all dreams. With enough elbow grease, you can probably make them happen. Will it suck? Yes. Could you do it? Well, barring a horrifying congenital soap allergy or what-have-you … yes.

On the other hand, "Get famous," "Make millions" and "Lord it over Samantha because that jerk has had it coming for *years*" are all byproducts. They may happen, but not on their own, not without first accomplishing an actual *goal*. And they're often fairly soulless.

The problem with byproducts is they are so directionless as to seriously hinder your ability to get there at all.

Plus, they're basically the antithesis of getting the hell over it. They keep you locked in place for years, making life decisions based on what will impress others, show them up or pad your ego. Unfortunately, though, very few success stories are built on a foundation of stickin' it to someone. It's just not the way to go, my creative friend.

So, to recap:

Dreams are pure, attainable visions.

Fantasies are fun, beautiful, fantastic, even salacious, but ultimately unrealizable illusions.

Byproducts are results that follow real action.

I've realized over time that I can only control a dream, something I can plan for, build on, work at, develop, share and nurture. I cannot do that with a fantasy, nor can I assure a byproduct except through hard work on a dream.

Even when I *do* set my heart on something that can be accomplished, I often stumble when it comes to actually executing it ... because I get in my own way. I get caught in my head. I think about all the things that could go wrong instead of the things that could go right.

The subject of the rest of this book will be taking your dream and learning to think about it the right way, learning to work without fear and just plain ol' getting the hell over it. As discussed.

First, though, take a moment to put your vision through the wringer. Where does it land? Is it a true dream? Is it even *worth* marshaling the resources you'll need to fight fear and succeed? I hope the answer is yes, but if not, it's best to find out now.

So you can get back to that Ryan Gosling thing.

Exercise:

Now think about the dream(s) you listed in the first exercise. Would you consider each a real dream you that you can attain, a fantasy that probably isn't going to happen or a byproduct that you should set aside in favor of working on a *real* dream?

III.
Career or Hobby? Or: Will This Make Me Put an Axe Through My Head?

Realism is not a strong suit for many people. It certainly isn't for me.

You'd think, as a successful creative, my approach to life and career would be direct, intentional and decisive.

Mmmmm, no. Not even a little bit. Honestly, I give waffling a new name.

It's taken me a long time to accept that writing is my calling (despite *first* realizing it at the age of 5, when I told my mom I was going to be a writer for a living). In between my writing phases, I've been a designer, a teacher, a would-be reporter and a banker. I've done brief stints as a painter, a photographer, a book reviewer and a chandler. (That's "candlemaker," to you new-fashioned folks.)

Uh ... you're thinking. *It doesn't really sound like you should be giving me career advice.*

Fair enough. However, I would argue that I'm in the best possible position to advise on this subject, because I've had so very long to examine firsthand the difference between *careers* and *hobbies*.

One of the most common mistakes people make when trying to decide whether or not to pursue creative endeavors is to assume that our hobbies should be a full-time occupation.

This isn't always, or even usually, true.

Often our hobbies don't translate well to careers.

A particularly salient example is that of one of my best friends. We'll call her Jane.

Jane is a teacher during the day. A few years ago, though, she was really struggling: the market was crappy, and she'd had no luck finding a job, despite the fact that she was three years out of grad school.

Jane also had a side business baking cakes and cupcakes for friends and family. She is FREAKING EXCELLENT at this, devoting a huge chunk of her off hours to mixing, frosting, rolling fondant, making tiny toppers and generally being a cake genius.

It was easy to come to the conclusion that Jane should open a bakery. The economy would have supported it, she wasn't having a ton of luck in the teaching world and she's crazy good.

Her answer?

"I wouldn't want to do it for a living."

In my opinion, Jane is smarter than most. She refused to make the mistake of thinking that enjoying something in her off-hours means she would enjoy it 40 hours a week, or, let's be honest, the 60 hours most creatives work.

Yet many of us conflate a *passionate hobby* with a *career passion*.

In fact, I myself got a master's degree in education under the erroneous impression that loving kids and having fond memories of being a camp counselor equated to wanting a classroom.

Nope. Now I write for a living. At home. Alone. All day. (See the difference there?)

So how can you avoid the same mistake I made? By thinking deeply about your creative love.

This isn't as easy as it sounds. We humans tend to be very bad at predicting what will make us happy. In fact, in any study of affective forecasting (our ability to predict how we will feel about any given event in the future), humans routinely perform terribly when it comes to predicting their own future feelings. To be fair, we're pretty good at this in the short term, as Timothy D. Wilson and Daniel T. Gilbert conclude in an article entitled *Affective Forecasting*:

> People are skilled at predicting the valence of their future emotional reactions; if the choice is between going out to dinner or watching dogs be euthanized at the local animal shelter, most people would know which activity would be fun and which would not. People are also skilled at guessing the specific kinds of emotional reactions they will have, such as predicting whether an insult from a co-worker is more likely to cause anger, fear, or disgust.

Good points. So far, so good. But when it comes to further in the future and longer-term feelings, we kinda suck:

> By far the most common error is the impact bias, the tendency to overestimate the enduring impact that future events will have on our emotional reactions. One reason for the impact bias is focalism, whereby people fail to anticipate the extent to which unrelated events will influence their thoughts and emotions, and thus overestimate the impact of the event they are considering.

This means two things for our purposes. First, that you can't safely assume something you kinda like right now will make for a good career. Second, and more importantly, *you should not assume that trying something and failing will be nearly as painful as you think it will be.*

It won't. You'll get over it. I swear, and I'm speaking as someone who had a book deal within her grasp and lost it (but that's a story for another time). Failures are painful, but they are very rarely fatal. You're not Napoleon, for God's sake. You're just you, and screwing something up isn't going to impact your life that much.

Trust me.

So if you think you've got a skill that will make for a good career, why not give it a go? You don't have to jump in headfirst; you're allowed to start small and do it on the side. The side of a 9-to-5, the side of raising kids or the side of a different creative passion. It's really all about what works for you, and it really doesn't have to be an instant win. You might hate it, and then give up. Cool! You tried!

That is the heart of getting the hell over it: not caring about results. Going for the dream while it's still a dream, and forgetting about the byproducts you hope to achieve. Because results don't matter.

Well, I suppose if you have $100,000 of startup capital from investors, they matter. But chances are good that, if that's the case, you're not reading this book.

Similarly, if your spouse has agreed to your quitting your job and pursuing this business idea, then again, it matters. So be sure before you do that that your dream actually *is* career-worthy. It sucks to find out afterward that it isn't. (Again, believe me.)

For the most part, though, the stakes are low.

So ask yourself: Why not try out a hobby and see if it's a career? Why not give your career idea a go, and see if it works for you? What's *really* at stake?

Exercise:

Use the space below to think about whether your dreams would make good full-time work or should just remain hobbies. Alternatively, think about whether some of these ideas would make good *side* businesses – bringing in a little income but not replacing your real work.

IV.
What's In Your Wheelhouse? Or: Discovering Your Dream

Here's a question that too many people fail to ask themselves, because they're afraid of the answer:

What's my dream?

To someone who has a burning, driving, all-consuming, hotter-than-the-fire-of-a-thousand-suns passion, this question will seem absolutely ludicrous. They feel it in their bones:

I've just got to do That One Thing.

It doesn't matter what that thing is; they've always known it was for them. Had to be. Nothing else could possibly take its place.

For me, that was writing. For others, it's painting or illustration or woodworking or graphic design.

This doesn't describe everyone, though. Lots of people are creative and *do* know they want to make, develop, produce for a living ... but simply have no idea what form it would take. They want to use their hands and find autonomy and get away from their day jobs, but that's about all they know.

If you feel this way, that's legitimate.

Sometimes the urge to create in general is more powerful than the urge to make something specific.

Also, lots of creative people are good at multiple things. You might be a great writer, but also really rock at decorating hatboxes, embossing stuff and taxidermy. And it's really hard to choose.

Because I mean ... hatboxes and taxidermy. That's some serious apples and oranges shit. Who knows, man?

There's a reason for this. We humans are weird animals, and choosing is *hard*. For one thing, making choices requires precious bodily resources (chief among them glucose, which you can read more about in one of my favorite books, *Willpower: Rediscovering the Greatest Human Strength*).

For another, when you choose you are essentially "killing off the other options," which we find psychologically uncomfortable. All choices require sacrifices.

In point of fact, the harder a decision becomes, the easier it actually *should* be to make. Why? Because if a choice is really, really hard, it means that the two options are so close together as to represent an almost meaningless difference between them. But we don't see this situation as easy as that.

Because what if that other option was the golden egg? What if?

Well, that's a risk you'll have to take. The alternative is bouncing around so often you'll never get settled anywhere. Cal Newport advocates this in another of my favorite books, *So Good They Can't Ignore You: Why Skills Trump Passion in the Quest for Work You Love*. His basic argument is that in a match between skill and passion, go for skill. If you're already good at something ... try to make that your dream.

But don't forget about the whole passion thing. Because while skill might trump it, having both is ideal.

So choose. Make sure it's feasible, or you'll just end up banging your head against the wall. In a race between several appealing opportunities, choose the one you're least likely to get burnt-out on. If possible, embrace the thing that really blows your hair back. It can only help.

And stop fretting.

So many people I know just can't *get over it and move on* because they're so afraid they're going to choose wrong. They think they'll accidentally choose the thing they'll end up failing at or the thing that others will find boring or unglamorous or the thing they maybe kinda *could* be good at but have failed at in the past.

This is stuff and nonsense. Seriously. *This* kind of thinking right here is what separates the ladies from the girls, the men from the boys, and the older non-gender-specified people from the younger non-gender-specified people. Who *cares* if you fail or bore others? Does that really change anything in your life? Anything real, anyway?

The answer is a hard no.

Now, I know. Fear and all that. I've been there, and we'll talk about that more in the next chapter.

For the moment, remember this: if you're lucky – and most of us are – life is a pretty long thing. If you set your mind to it, you can write multiple books, launch five businesses, create various types of crafts and/or raise a bunch of children *while* nurturing a creative business. These are all totally possible routes, so don't stress about the idea of simply choosing one for now. You'll get there.

Settle on a dream. Really dig into what it means to achieve it. Read the rest of this book and give it the ol' college try. Maybe it works. Maybe it doesn't. Refuse to give a f***, and if you have to, try something new.

Still need help figuring out what you might like to do? Questions to the rescue!

Exercise:

Many creative people languish wanting to do something but not knowing what. Should they paint? Cook? Make fairy houses? Invent weird new uses for old shoes? Luckily, open-ended inquiry is an excellent window into the soul. If you feel stuck, spend some time answering the following questions.

Without further ado, here are 25 questions to get your creative juices flowing about ... well ... creativity:

1) What do you do when you're alone?

2) Where have you been when you've experienced your biggest aha moments?

3) What's your favorite blog?

4) What room of your house do you go to for comfort?

5) Name three things you love to make.

6) What's the best handmade gift you've ever made for someone?

7) How do you feel about the holidays?

8) Should *The Lord of the Rings* involve more baking?

9) Do you have a bulletin board? Why or why not? (There is only one answer to this question: You need a bulletin board.)

10) List your top ten favorite colors. YES, TEN OF THEM.

11) Which do you think is more important: uniqueness or consistency?

12) What's your favorite thing your mom ever made for you?

13) Do you like to please other people, or could you not care less?

14) How do you feel about social media?

15) What is your favorite pattern?

16) Does Martha Stewart make you happy or suicidal?

17) What makes you lose track of time, makes you stop thinking, eating, sleeping, talking because all you want is to do that one thing?

18) Who inspires you the most?

19) Do you judge books by their covers?

20) What is your favorite animal? (Mythological totally acceptable ... preferred, even.)

21) If your creative work were a food, what would it be?

22) Coffee or tea?

23) Where do you feel inspiration physically (in your head, hands, heart, elsewhere)?

24) What do you turn to when you're upset? Books? Photos? The outdoors? Your closet? Your trusty KitchenAid?

25) What kind of work are you proud to share with others?

V.
Living and Working Without Fear, Or: Quit Crying Into Your Horoscope

You know that feeling you get? When you're just trying to drink a morning cup of coffee and get a little business development done, and instead you end up crying into your horoscope because *why, why, why and when will it all end and haven't you paid your dues by now and oh, the fear! THE FEAR! BECAUSE WHAT WILL PEOPLE THINK?*

Or something like that?

Sound … familiar-ish?

No, me neither. Because I am unshakeable and courageous, and such thoughts would never cross my mind.

Except that one time.

See, I have a story to tell. It's a short story but one I think you'll appreciate and maybe even empathize with.

This is the story of my overwhelming fear, a while ago, when the work I'd been doing since grad school started to fall through. At about the same time, I split with my agent before we could work out the book deal I'd so cherished the thought of. To round things out, I was six months pregnant with pneumonia and a broken rib.

Fun!

No, wait. It was HORRIBLE. I felt imprisoned all the time inside a First-World Iron Maiden of the mind, tortured by my failures and insecurities. While I desperately wanted to keep working for myself in order to be home with my kids, I didn't see how that was going to happen.

I almost gave up.

But my husband didn't let me. To my everlasting love and gratitude, he believed in my abilities and in me, even when I didn't. He told me I should start my own business, the one I'd been hesitating to put out there for years.

I made the change. Now I'm so happy I could burst.

The thing is, I let fear rule me for too long.

Once I realized that's what was happening, I resolved to put a stop to it. I read everything I could get my hands on about confidence, self-esteem, courage and boldness. Sometimes it didn't feel like enough, but I kept reading.

One day I woke up and had the novel thought:

Huh. I don't care that I'm afraid anymore.

I really didn't. I still felt fear, yes, and I still heard that awful voice (especially at night) whispering to me that I *couldn't do it* and that it *wouldn't work*, but I no longer *cared*. I was all, "Hey voice, what up?" And then I went back to sleep.

Magical.

And then, even better, I woke up a month or so later and realized:

I'm not afraid today.

I'd been through the wringer, trying to figure out who I was and what I wanted. The crucible of desperation had washed me out, leaving me clean and cured and ready to work and believe at all costs.

That's where I am now, and it feels awesome. But I'm no fool.

The fear will be back.

It always is. The trick is acceptance, understanding that even though you're afraid, you still have cause to believe in yourself. If you truly want to get the hell over it and live a meaningful, creative life, you have to expect that fear and decide it doesn't matter all that much.

Because really, who cares? None of it is real. After all:

The main difference between a day when you feel like you could conquer the world and a day when you feel like the world is grinding you under its heel is nothing but a few chemicals in your brain.

And they don't get to be in charge.

The best approach to managing your fears is first understanding them, which isn't as hard as you think. Fears come in five basic categories:

1) Extinction

2) Mutilation

3) Loss of autonomy

4) Separation

5) Ego-death

If you're like me, your first response to this list is ... whoa. Just ... whoa. Let's all just *calm down here*. But they make sense when you break them down.

In layman's terms, we fear ceasing to exist, coming to harm, being confined or limited, losing connectedness or being rejected, and suffering a blow to the ego.

Although "extinction" might sound a little extreme, it's a fear many people experience daily. When you imagine quitting your day job to start your own business and you feel that rush of anxiety, that's an extinction fear: *If the job doesn't work out, how will you pay the bills, eat, exist?*

The embarrassment we worry we'll feel when we launch a blog and nobody reads it is both separation and ego-death. We fear isolation from our peers and making a fool of ourselves. We fear being run out of the group because we broke the rules and it's not okay.

These aren't crazy – in fact, in terms of evolutionary biology, they make a lot of sense – but they are irrational. The most common fears I hear about and experience are as follows:

1) I can't do it.

2) It won't work out.

3) Everyone will laugh at me.

4) There's no market for this.

5) I'm not ready yet.

And the answers, folks, are simpler than you might think:

1) You *can* do it. Look at all the successful businesses out there. The ideas that took off. The artists making a living. Are you really less functional or saleable than *all of those people*? I don't think so.

2) It will if you work hard enough.

3) No, they won't. They care way more about protecting their *own* egos than going after yours. As for the few who do laugh ... screw them, man.

4) There's a market for everything. Like, *everything*. Go look up the weirdest thing you can think of on Google. Oh, look! There it is!

5) And when will you be ready? In ten years when you've been telling yourself that for ... ten years?

You see my point. Fears are little jerks. Bullies. You just gotta talk back.

Plus, we radically underestimate the importance of failure. No, seriously, that's not a trite platitude. Failure is crucial to success, teaching us to forge ahead, keep going, thicken our hides and persist even in the face of overwhelming disapproval or disbelief. We just don't know that, because the data on failure disappears.

So stop living in fear. It's just another way of trying to divine the future: if this, then that; if *this*, then *that*. It's pointless. Stop. Stop.

Just stop.

Instead of letting fear rule you, write down a few things you're afraid of. Then, after each fear, write down your new stock responses.

For instance, you might write, "I'm afraid of my high school classmates seeing my blog and thinking it's stupid." (Note: Some of us in our 30s are still afraid of stuff like that, so it's totally fine to feel that way and even better to admit it, because then you can actually deal with it in a healthy way!)

Your answer might be, "I won't let others' judgment dampen my courage." Then, whenever you're afraid of former classmates seeing your work, just remind yourself that *they're* not putting anything out into the world and *you* are. Or maybe they are, and it's good, and possibly much better than what you're doing, but ... so? Someone is always better than you. It doesn't freaking matter.

And so on. Give it a shot.

Exercise:

1) Write down a few of your main fears.

2) Write down your answers to them.

3) Practice those answers over and over again, until you start to believe them. It will take time, but it will happen.

4) Enjoy the bliss that comes with giving fewer f***s about what other people think of you.

VI.
Relying On Yourself, Or: OMG Stop Asking for Attention

Relying on yourself is hard.

We don't *want* to rely on ourselves. We want others to make us feel nice and cozy, to stand by our sides and champion us when we just can't do it for ourselves. We want them to fill the Endless Void of Raging Terrible Emotion that constantly hollows out our insides.

It's a brutal place in there, amiright?

But see, that's no one's job but yours. Because the truth is, no matter *how* much love and energy someone pours into your soul, it will never be enough if you can't rely on yourself.

For example, consider my Instagram account. It's pretty good. I like it. It's gone through changes over the years, but for the most part, it brings me joy and gives me a platform for talking about books and writing, which I love and appreciate.

Back when I started, though, it was an exercise in agony. *Because no one noticed.*

I had taken a class. I worked hard to craft lovely photos. I put up three posts a day. But nothing happened.

We've all been here: poured our hearts and souls into something and flung it into the ether, only to hear crickets in return. In some ways, this is worse than abject failure. At least when the Universe gives you a solid DEAR GOD, SARAH, *NO* ... well, you have your answer.

But silence? It's truly unsettling. We hate it. We want to feel like we're awesome *now* and feel utterly betrayed when we put time and effort into something and don't immediately get the adoration we feel we deserve.

Well, get over it. Only your mom and dad think you're a success just because you exist, and if they're good parents, you don't even get *that* much adoration.

Good. Because your job is to learn to rely on yourself to feel okay about not *yet* being as successful as you'd like.

The truth is, we feel like failures *until* we're successes, and this is the wrong approach. You need to learn to think of the interim not as a big ol' F, but as a time during which you are not *yet* successful.

This is the point at which most of us turn to others for validation and comfort. But resist the urge. It isn't your friends' or family's job to be your constant cheerleaders. If you get a few kudos, count yourself lucky. These peeps are busy working on their lives, and a following composed entirely of your friends is pretty meaningless anyway. You already had that following, and they ain't going to make your business happen.

That doesn't mean it won't sting when they don't seem to notice or care what you do. But again, get the hell over it.

You need to get used to showing up and doing the work without applause.

It's the people who have this skill who truly succeed in their lives and businesses.

So get started. Make your products. Blog. Market yourself. Advertise. Get business cards. Build websites. Start referring to yourself with a job title that reflects what you do. Don't feel like you deserve it yet? Too bad. Grab your balls/ovaries/whatever you like to grab, and call yourself that anyway.

And if you're just starting out, it's okay not to say anything. After all, in the beginning, telling other people about your goals can actually work against you. Seems odd, I know, but research dating as far back as the 1920s indicates that shouting your dreams from the rooftops may actually make you less likely to achieve them, possibly because just sharing your goals gives you a feeling of accomplishment that makes you less likely to work on them.

Weak. Sauce.

I know. But keep it in mind for the early stages. If you haven't yet created your products, put up that website, started that social media channel or otherwise launched, you might want to keep those plans to yourself. Not forever, but for a bit.

And for God's sake, stop wallowing in failure. It's just another way of asking for attention, and no one likes it. (I feel like you might get tired of me saying this, but ... trust me.)

Yet many of us do this, mainlining self-help blogs like they're crack and mumbling how much we suck into bottles of wine. Pointless.

Now that you mention it, actually, this is *exactly* like crack: an expensive waste of your time, brain and emotional energy.

So just stop. Learn to rely on yourself. When fear crops up and you want to run to your boyfriend/ girlfriend/mom/granddad/whoever, just stop, take a deep breath and acknowledge the fear. Give it a little wave. Invite it over for cocktails at five o'clock, but make it clear that you're busy right now.

Be firm.

Now, one caveat.

This doesn't mean you shouldn't let the world know how great you are when the situation actually calls for it, though.

I remember one time my father-in-law was telling my husband he should get a secretary (they both do taxes), and my husband said we couldn't afford it. Pops said, "So hire Sarah." On the one hand, it was flattering that he thought I could wrap my head around taxes even in a secretarial role.

On the other hand … *what the hell?* I was a successful businesswoman! I had lots of clients! I made MORE money than my husband!

But he just didn't *know*. I hadn't said anything, so how could he? Everyone assumed I still just sort of flailed along like I always had. There was a long period of time during which *nothing* I tried proved successful, and in response, I'd developed a fear of and aversion to talking about my "business" at all. That fear sealed my mouth shut, so that I never came out once I *was* successful and told people. My father-in-law couldn't have known.

Which means that other people – potential clients, customers, mentors and business partners – couldn't have known either.

Booooooooooooooooo.

So when you've earned some praise, put your successes out there, and don't worry about being judged.

Will it happen sometimes? I mean, yeah. But in all honesty, how much time do you spend judging others for their self-promotion? Are you ever like: *Oh my GOD, is she doing it AGAIN? Trying to get people to JOIN HER FACEBOOK GROUP? What, does she want to be SUCCESSFUL or something? How DARE she assume we care about her very human dreams and aspirations.*

No. You *never* think that. At least, I hope you don't do that, because that would make you kind of an asshole. You probably just immediately click away, forget about it and go check on the macaroni and cheese. Because you're living your life. Chances are, though, if you even notice, you're kinda like, "Cool, bro. You do you."

Moreover, once you stop judging others, you'd be surprised how much less fear you have about getting judged yourself. It just sort of evaporates.

You might be surprised by how easy this all is, too. Believe it or not, if you just make the decision to stop asking for attention, fearing every step you take, and judging others/fearing judgment yourself, *you'll have a lot more time to create.*

If you use that time wisely, you'll earn the respect and attention you deserve *organically*, without having to hook others into your sad schemes.

It's such a better way to live life, and I know you can get there.

Exercise:

There's only one exercise for this section, and it's this: Practice putting something online that scares you and then *not giving a shit* what comes of it. This can be as simple as a Facebook or blog post, a tweet or an Instagram photo that shares a little something about your business. That's it. Check out the comments if you want, but most importantly: Just get it up there.

Then do it again.

And again.

And again.

That's called building a business, my friend. You got this.

VII.
Teaching Yourself With Courage, Or: Who Cares If It Doesn't Work?

So you've decided on your dream career or hobby. You've determined it a worthwhile goal and you're not going to let fear stop you.

This is often where creatives get stuck.

You're past that initial firestorm of joy – *Yes, that! That's my passion! I'll do it no matter what, goldangit, and nothing and no one is EVER GONNA STOP ME* – and now you have to figure out what the hell to do about it.

Ugh. Gross.

Often, the biggest problem is we just don't yet know how to do That Thing We Want to Do.

So we just kinda ... go for it. Which isn't as good (or as courageous) an approach as you might think.

Now, I'm all for the "ready, fire, aim" methodology, which says that you just need to point your gun *somewhere* in the vicinity of your target. You can fine-tune and add the glossy details later. But this isn't the same as launching with no knowledge of what needs to be done. Not sure what I'm talking about? Here's a little word picture I love:

*"The metaphor that comes up for me when I work with many small creative businesses is that of **a little boat in the middle of the ocean. Happily working along, making some sales, going where the wind is going.***

"But the problem is that when there is a big wave or a storm brewing, they are not prepared.

"And they struggle.

"There is no direction.

"There is no harbour they are aiming for.

"Nobody is really 'in charge.'"

Yes, even in a biz of one, you can't lack a person in charge. Why? Because fear is struggling for the leadership role, and more often than you'd like ... you let fear win.

Like I said, this is neither a good nor courageous approach.

However, at *some* point, you will need to just get started. And that's where teaching yourself your craft comes in. Ideally, you'll have some foundational knowledge in the industry, but there's absolutely no way you'll know *everything*, so you're going to have to get that knowledge another way.

By teaching yourself.

"Okay!" we think gamely. "Time to become an expert! Time to get all awesome at what we do and ROCK THE WORLD!"

Then we pick up books like Malcolm Gladwell's *Outliers* and it all comes crumbling down. "CRAP," we despair. "Where am I *ever* going to find 10,000 hours to become an expert?"

We begin to panic. How can we possibly teach ourselves something new with jobs, kids and life to deal with? We haven't even gotten around to buying kibble yet ... and we've been feeding the dog Campbell's soup for three weeks already. It just won't work, right?

Many people end their love affairs with a dream here, but they shouldn't.

Granted, if you're hoping to get hired somewhere for your creative genius, you'll need skills and a killer portfolio at the very least. Often you won't be considered without a degree, in which case learning your chosen trade better be something you're *very* serious about. But this doesn't mean you have to be an expert.

Besides, you don't have to go that route.

I think you're going to guess what I have to say here:

It's time to get the hell over it.

It's time to move past the stupid belief that you have to be the best at what you do before you can launch your business. It's time to rustle up the skills and capital you do have, and forget about what you lack. Then put it all to work for you.

Look: It doesn't take a degree to launch a blog or an Etsy site. It doesn't take a degree to experiment. You just need willingness and, to be honest, some innate talent. If you've got those, you've got the makings of a successful dream.

Now it's time to make your peace with potential failure, recognize its value, invite it in, scrounge up some time and GO.

One of the best approaches is rapid skill acquisition, a technique advocated by Josh Kaufman in his book *The First 20 Hours: How to Learn Anything ... Fast*.

This is a novel approach to learning a new technique that limits the time and effort necessary to teach yourself something new, and therefore lessens the associated fear.

That's because rapid skill acquisition doesn't mean mastering the skill.

It means learning it *well enough* to make a decision about whether or not you should pursue it. If you love it and show talent, awesome; you've invested very little time to discover that your dream is both feasible and enjoyable.

If not, meh. Take a little break, lick your superficial wounds (and they ARE superficial), then try again.

Once you hit on that perfect possibility, you'll know it.

Time to get serious.

Self-education can feel overwhelming. There are no built-ins. No professors. No syllabi. No ready-made roster of study buddies. No books list. No assignments. No demos. No feedback.

You have to find everything on your own.

This isn't as hard as it sounds.

If you take your dream seriously, you can find both like-minded creatives (study buddies) and mentors (professors) online or in person. Books and assignments abound; you just get to choose them for yourself. Friends, family and readers can all provide great feedback. As for a syllabus, you get to choose that too; you get to do whatever you want – awesome, right?

Your approach can take several forms:

1) Building a portfolio
2) Amassing a selection of offerings for sale
3) Compiling a list of services
4) Starting a blog

Your dream will determine which route you take.

If you want to get published, for instance, a blog is the way to go. Artists need portfolios, and so on. Once you decide your end product, you can break it down into smaller chunks and work toward it, essentially creating a syllabus for yourself.

As for demos, you've got no excuse. The world is *awash* in free tutorials, people.

For instance, you can look up pretty much anything on YouTube. Seriously, almost anything. Want to learn how to tie rad sailor's-knots? YouTube. Skin and fricassee frog legs? YouTube. How to kiss? YouTube, baby! (Though it's hard to see how you'll make a business out of that, I will be very much interested if you do. Godspeed.)

You can also learn a wide variety of media-related skills on Lynda.com.

Or you can hit up iTunes or various websites to take advantage of the thousands upon thousands of free or low-cost tutorials offered by other creatives.

It's all out there. You just have to find it.

And the whole time you're doing it, *you get to practice getting over it*. When you feel so overwhelmed your heart feels like it's going to eat your ribcage and escape your chest, practice getting over it. When you feel as though you're a failure already, get over it. When you can't get your real-life product to match the vision in your head, GET THE HELL OVER IT, MY FRIEND.

Keep going. Keep learning.

Always.

Exercise:

Feeling overwhelmed? Use the space below to write down what you need to learn to make your business a reality. Then break that into the smallest possible steps. For instance, "I need to learn how to sell my paintings on Etsy!" should become:

1) Create an Etsy profile.

2) Take photos of my work or figure out who will take them for me.

3) Write product descriptions.

4) Enroll in an Etsy marketing course (if necessary).

5) What does your process look like? You don't need to have *accomplished* every step; you just need to write them down and get to work a little bit at a time.

6) Don't be a weenie. Do it.

VIII.
Finding Your Tools, Or: This Paintbrush Sucks

Y ou can't do good work without good tools. That's just a fact.

Usually when you're pulling yourself up by your bootstraps, however, you don't have the resources to invest in every lovely tool you'd like to have. Scraping together the bare necessities might even feel like too much. For now, you just have to let go of crazy shit like this.

I mean seriously, WHAT.

But for now? No.

I was lucky: I got a journalism degree and came out of my program with most of what I needed to start a business: Computer, camera, software, skillz.

Yet everywhere I look, I see some ah-MAZING program/gadget/tool I would give my eyeteeth to own. So many, many, many things that would make me a better writer, if only I could spend ten life savings' worth of money and –

Oh wait, too bad.

The people who own those tools are either independently wealthy or, much more likely, much further along in their careers. Chances are good that when *they* were starting out, they didn't have such swanky tools either.

Often, though, that's not something we choose to recognize. We just assume we *have* to have these things in order to "do a good job."

The problem with this is we tend to wait until we have the ideal setup before starting.

Unfortunately, it's unlikely that if you sit around and wait, you will somehow amass all the capital and all the paraphernalia comprising that optimal arrangement.

So what can you do?

Well, the first step is to take stock of what you *do* have. At a bare minimum, anyone hoping to launch a creative dream needs:

1) Space: Somewhere to work
2) Time: A window in which to work
3) Network: Someone to show your work to
4) Colleagues: People to talk shop with
5) Supplies: Enough to get started

First things first: **Space**. We're not talking a glorious studio with parquet floors and east-facing windows here. You just need somewhere to work, preferably uninterrupted by children or *Law & Order: SVU*. Your basement; your garage; the mudroom. Try to add a few beautiful elements if possible so that you look forward to coming into your space.

You also need **Time**. A big enough chunk that you can actually dig in and do deep work. For people with day jobs and children, this often means early in the morning or late at night. Perhaps a lunch break or a blocked-out Sunday. Whatever it is, make it happen.

A **Network** allows you to get your work out there once you produce it. It took me a long time to learn that I didn't have to have a million amazing connections to have a network. Friends, family, people in your graduating class, the barista you really like ... these people are all in your network. Tell them about your work; you never know what will strike a chord or who they might tell.

Colleagues are simply people with whom you can discuss your creative endeavors; people who are doing similar work to yours. *The good news is you don't have to know them first.* Bloggers and authors both count as colleagues, and you never know who's willing to become your friend until you ask. I've made lots of friends online. Some of those friends have become close colleagues or lifelong buddies.

I hope, anyway. You never know when someone's going to go insane, let out all the animals at their local zoo and go to prison for life.

But for now? Yeah, they rule.

And lastly, **Supplies**. This is what often trips folks up, but it shouldn't. Social media, email and blogs are all free. You don't need to own a digital camera to post pictures of your work. You can ask a friend to borrow theirs, or use your phone. You can find amazing stock images for less than $15 if you use Canva.

When it comes to the physical tools of your trade, look for the substitutes: If you're a painter, do you really need more than some acrylic paints and a couple of paintbrushes to create a portfolio? I would argue no; people will either recognize the unique spirit of your paintings, or they won't.

Blick paints and squirrel-hair brushes aren't going to change that.

Sorry, but it's true. Get over it.

And get to work.

Exercise:

What you really need is a plan for how you're going to make do until you *do* have every tool under the sun. One day, if you're serious about what you want to do, you'll get there. For now, write down the bare minimum of supplies you need. Be realistic, but be harsh, especially if you're on a budget.

IX.
Defining Your Niche, Or: You Are What You Offer

As creative individuals, we love to do many things. It's a rare artist, for instance, that can't dabble in multiple media. Musicians can also write. Writers often make a living in journalism or copywriting but long to produce fiction.

Being a Renaissance man or woman is all well and good, but unfortunately, people don't care about your many skills, passions, hobbies, interests and thoughts.

You have to know what *they* need.

Because they're coming to you for one thing. That one thing you're good at.

That one thing you do better than everyone else.

It doesn't have to be a big thing. You don't always have to stick to it. But you have to know what it *is*. And to do that you need to know your niche. Or more specifically, your target audience.

Of course, if you only care about pursuing your creative dream as a hobby, you don't care so much about this. But *most* people with a burning desire to make something happen don't want a hobby, so this is highly relevant.

Case study:

My target audience used to read something like: *Anyone looking for illustration, web design or writing, come on down!*

That's not going to cut it. People look at that and say, "I bet I can find someone better."

And they're right. Anyone purporting to be awesome at three gargantuan, unspecified categories is a liar. They will always lose out to the expert who specializes in just one, or better yet, a small subset of one.

Niche it down.

After a bunch of tedious work and soul-searching, my niche now reads: *I write creative copy and content for young creatives, entrepreneurs and small businesses.*

I only do three main kinds of writing – email news-letters, blog posts and web copy, and ads. I also limit my audience, because typically people can't pay my rates when they're younger than 25 (at a minimum), and those who are older than 65 are usually super out-of-touch with digital, which is my main medium.

Now I can define my niche with the following parameters:

» Age group (youngish, but not too young)

» Type (few to no big businesses)

» Ethic (small and personal)

» Services (copywriting and content marketing)

So I now have a much better idea of who I'm looking for, and will have a much easier time getting inside their heads because of it.

But can they pay?

This is an important question.

To answer it, I like Ramit Sethi's Pay Certainty Technique, a very simple metric for whether or not your idea has value. Answer two questions about your ideal client:

» Do they have the ability to pay?

» Do they have the willingness to pay?

In my case, I believe the answer to both questions is yes. My ideal client is already established, so they can afford me. They are also willing to pay, because they care about eloquence and clarity, and want to present their own goods and services to the world as beautifully as possible.

Boom.

There are, however, less saleable ideas. At first look, for instance, you might think it's a great idea to give personal finance lessons to inner-city children. There's a decent chance they don't get a lot of that in their home and school environments, and it could make a huge difference in their lives.

But here's where the Pay Certainty Technique comes in: Even if they or their parents had the willingness to pay for lessons that could prove truly valuable, there's a good chance they can't afford them. You're better off offering these services on a volunteer basis and looking for your bread 'n' butter elsewhere.

It can go the other way as well. Just the other day, someone asked me if I needed editing services, and I was like ... why would anyone even ask me that? I'm a professional writer and I have been for years. Obviously I a) don't need one at all, or b) have found an editor already. (The answer happens to be b.)

Sure, I could pay the editor who solicited me. But I'm not going to. I lack the willingness because it's not a service I am in need of right now. Editors are better off seeking audiences *outside* the writing world, because those people much less capable themselves and much more likely to need the service.

So before you launch, scrutinize your intended product:

» Does it withstand the Pay Certainty test?

» Do people actually want it?

» Have you niched it down?

» Will you be happy providing this product for the foreseeable near future?

» Does it represent you to your core?

This matters. You are what you offer.

The following exercise will help you dig deep to find that perfect target audience.

Exercise:

Here are a few questions to ask yourself to help determine whether or not your product is saleable:

1) Have you seen this product somewhere else? (If so, that's actually a good sign.)

2) Have you seen this product *everywhere* else? (If so, that might be a bad sign, unless you do it really, really well.)

3) Has anyone already in your audience mentioned wanting this product?

4) What *have* people you know mentioned wanting?

5) Are your products priced relatively similarly to other products in your niche?

6) Will you be able to scale this product or service once your business is bigger? In other words, if your business explodes, can you see making this product a thousand at a time rather than two at a time? Or offering this service to a point where you are doing it full time?

7) If not, what could you do to make scaling your business easier later?

8) What extras can you offer along with your product to help it sell? (A cute bookmark, an exclusive Facebook community, a discount code.)

9) Are you willing to work hard to market your product in your niche? (If you are too shy or lazy, I'm sorry, but it just won't do well, so save yourself the heartache.)

10) DO YOU KNOW WHAT PROBLEM THIS PRODUCT SOLVES? (This is the most important question of all, because whether you sell a good or a service, you need to be able to tell people WHY they want it. Spend extra time making sure you know this answer.)

X.
Design Time, Or: Are You Sure Anyone Wants to Look at That?

Of necessity, I'm going to start this short chapter with a disclaimer: I have a strong design background. I care a lot about how things look.

I think you should care too.

So yeah, I'm a little biased. But I'm also *right*.

Think about the last time you visited a travel website. Scanned a DIY blog. Perused a home improvement article. Yes, your eyes no doubt took in text – or some of it, at least – but the majority of your experience was likely comprised of conscious or unconscious scanning of images, sidebars, headers.

In other words, design.

Don't believe me? How long do you spend on university web pages? You know, the ones with grainy backgrounds and blocks of text in size 18, turquoise serif font? Yeah, *those* ones. Unless we're looking for something very, very special, we usually leave such websites shortly after we arrive.

And though we rarely think about it at the time, the reason is obvious:

We associate beauty with value.

That's why Etsy lists *taking beautiful photos* among its top suggestions for increasing your sales. That's why people pay for fancy logos instead of just slapping their initials up on web pages, billboards and business cards. And that's why *you* should care about the way you present yourself as well.

After all, would you put on your schlubby khakis and paint-splattered T-shirt before a job interview? Unless you're interviewing with a gang of street artists, probably not.

Your business or hobby deserves the same care and attention.

Because even if *you* think design is somehow "extra" or "superficial," I promise you your potential clients do not.

Especially if your business focuses on your creative abilities, your presentation tells your clients how to think of your product. You might make elaborate artisanal cutting boards lovingly cured with mineral oil over a period of three months, but if all prospective clients see is a canned WordPress theme without a lot of TLC, they'll leave.

So assuming you're not a designer, illustrator, photographer or otherwise-interested-in-graphic-arts type of person ... what can you do?

Among the easiest modifications you can make to your brand presence, especially online, are:

1) Get a logo. (Try this if you don't want to pay for it.)

2) Choose brand colors and use them consistently.

3) Choose a nice theme – WordPress, Tumblr, Shopify, Squarespace, etc. – for your blog or website. Modify it enough to distinguish it from the original; people do not notice the familiar, so try to make your presence *new*.

4) Put up a Facebook and Twitter header that showcases what you do.

5) Try to integrate your design into all pieces of your brand, including email marketing campaigns, business cards, online shops and brochures.

At this point, I want to make it *very, very clear* that you shouldn't expect this to be perfect. It takes time to develop a fabulous look, so be patient with yourself. You don't have to get it right on the first try, and in fact, you probably won't be happy with how things look the first few times around.

But beware: Many creatives spend undue amounts of time designing and redesigning instead of getting actual work done. This could be a sign you're avoiding your *real* tasks, and that fear has come back in one of its most common, and most insidious, forms: productive procrastination.

Don't let it.

Get the hell over your inclination toward perfectionism.

Instead, choose an aesthetic that works for you, then roll with it for a while. As your work matures, so will the way you dress it up, and that's okay.

Eventually you'll find your sweet spot, that place where you feel good in your skin, and people will start to notice.

That will be a good day. For now, write out your basic design plan, check those ideas off your list, and move on.

Exercise:

Make a SHORT list of the design-related tasks you'll need to complete in order to get your dream goin'. Then schedule them into your calendar and start checking them off one by one.

XI.
Selling Yourself, Or: Ewwww, Marketing ...

Marketing is crucial. Without it, you won't get anywhere. No one will learn your name. No one will buy your many amazing things. Your dreams will gather dust, and maybe your soul will too.

Is that what you want? Soul dust?

I didn't think so.

But here's the thing: I'm the last person on Earth who should be giving *anyone* marketing advice. I'm terrible at it; I'm super shy, and for most of my career I got the majority of my work through anonymous online sources that never saw my face.

That's how I prefer it, and for a long time I managed to convince myself this was a good thing. I'm a lone wolf! An individualist! I do my own thang!

But. But.

This strategy is good for one thing, and one thing only: stagnation.

It isn't going to help me grow a business. It isn't going to put me on good clients' radars. And it prevents me from practicing in public, which Seth Godin says is essential to getting better at your craft.

Still, marketing always felt so cheap. Whorish, even.

Somehow the phrase "selling yourself" is a little too close to the phrase ... "selling yourself." If you see what I mean.

It only took one sentence for me to change my mind.

At a meet-and-greet in my hometown, I had a chance to meet one of my heroes, Jeff Goins, one of the world's finest examples of a self-made digital creative. My first question for him was how he became comfortable marketing himself and using social media. He shrugged and uttered the words that changed my whole worldview:

Marketing isn't a bad thing.

It takes a moment to sink in, right?

But as soon as he said it, my fears began to fade. *Sharing ideas – your own as well as others' – is a completely legitimate use of time, energy and airwaves.* Besides, if we won't market ourselves, who will?

Sadly, our dreams often don't come true because *we simply don't ask folks to invest.*

You have to give people the option to care.

So first, decide to do it. Get over your fears. Spend some time in Chapter V if you need to. Talk to your mom. Cuddle your dog. Make this popcorn. Or any of these. Whatever.

Now get up and figure out how you're going to get yourself out there. Unfortunately, being hopeless is no excuse. Plenty of crash courses exist on topics such as:

» Social media

» Networking

» Starting a blog

» Building a great email list

... or even ... drum roll, please ...

Cold-calling!

Not that cold-calling ought to be your first resort, but hey, people still do it. Because it still works.

The key to marketing is to just try and be a normal human.

Tell a story. Share briefly. Invite cordially. Make people laugh. Give a gift. Introduce. Gain expertise.

Don't do anything you wouldn't do in the aisle of a grocery store.

And remember: Marketing isn't a bad thing.

Scary, yes.

Impossible? Nope.

Never. So get the hell over it, and just start doing it.

Exercise:

Write down the FIRST marketing strategy you're going to try, and stick with it until you're good at it. Then try something else. (Yes, just one strategy! Deal with it!)

XII.
Taking Names and Kicking Ass ... Whichever You Prefer

This is a short chapter. Don't say you weren't warned.

And here's why it's short: Only *you* know what kicking ass and taking names means.

It probably involves some version of doing what you've only been thinking about for years. It likely requires some hard, deep, killer, badass work (maybe while listening to this song). It certainly means kicking fear in the teeth.

And it absolutely, positively, under no circumstances involves Ryan Gosling.

Because that's ... what? Who knows what that is? Lady at the back? Yes! Correct!

That's a fantasy.

You have permission to engage in fantasies when your work is *over*, people. Until then, it is your job to understand what you want, refuse doubt, learn your trade, use the best tools you have and share what you make with the world.

In other words, to kick ass.

And take names.

You get where I'm going with this.

Okay, get out there and WIN AT CREATIVE LIFE! And be sure to email me if you have any questions, would like to see more specific information in the form of posts on the blog, or need anything else! I hope to hear from you soon.

(See? Told you it was a short chapter.)

About Me

My name is Sarah, but my friends call me
... Sarah. Sorry, I thought maybe I had
something more exciting to add there.

Guess not.

Anyway, I'm a design-loving book nerd who reads
whenever possible and writes for the thrill of it. Oh,
and also because it's my job.

If I've learned anything in the last five years of
running my own business and writing all day, it's
this: y'all, it just ain't as hard as it looks. Not the
business side and not the writing. If you want to
learn more about either, you can head to my courses
here and here.

A bit more about, you know, my credentials?
Well, okay: I have a master's degree in journalism
from Northwestern University and have worked

as a professional writer for the last six years. I am also certified as a specialist in fitness nutrition and possess a master's-level teaching degree. I'm the owner of the Instagram account @newleafwriter, where I chronicle my journeys in literature, life and obsessively arranging small items of home décor.

When I'm not hard at work writing, reading and reviewing, I'm playing with my two kids, doing yoga, cooking or compulsively rearranging my bookshelves.

Made in the USA
Middletown, DE
30 March 2021